The Green Street Three

Illustrated by Tina Holdcroft

Jaap Tuinman

CONSULTANTS
Anna Cresswell
Gail Heald-Taylor
Lynda Hodson
Glen Huser

ADVISER
Moira McKenzie

PROGRAMME EDITOR
Kathleen Doyle

Schofield & Sims Ltd
Educational Publishers

Journeys

Level Five
The Green Street Three

TEACHER CONTRIBUTORS
Barbara Currie
Jay Milne

ISBN 0-7217-0562-6

Printed and bound in England
ABCDEFGHIJ 9876543210

First printed 1985

Contents

GREEN ST

4

Carnival Costumes

By Sharon Siamon

D.J. liked joke books better than anything. He liked asking people the jokes and seeing them smile when he told them the funny answers.

One morning D.J. was taking his new book of pig jokes to school. He read some of the jokes to Lisa and Patti on the way.

"Why are pigs pink?" he asked.

"I don't know," said Lisa. "Why?"

"So you can tell them from oranges!" answered D.J. and they all laughed.

"Can I have a turn?" asked Patti. D.J. handed her the book. "Listen to this. How do you tell a boy pig from a girl pig?"

"How?" asked D.J.

"Call one up," read Patti. "If *he* answers, it's a boy; if *she* answers, it's a girl."

The three friends were still telling pig jokes when they got to school. As they walked down the hall, D.J. remembered that the skating carnival was next week. It had been so much fun last year! There had even been prizes for the best costumes.

5

"Do you have your carnival costumes yet?" he asked Patti and Lisa.

"I don't," said Patti.

"Remember that cow costume that Miss Mason and Mrs. O'Connor wore last time?" laughed Lisa. "They looked *so* funny!"

"This year I'm going to try for the Funniest Costume Prize," said D.J.

"Me too!" said Patti and Lisa together.

After school Lisa and Patti began to talk about the carnival again.

"We'll have to think of really funny costumes," said Lisa.

"But what?" asked Patti.

Just then D.J. came along. "Forget it," he told them with a big smile. "I'm going to win that prize. I'm going to have a really great costume."

"What is it?" asked Lisa.

"I'm not telling. It's a secret," said D.J. "I don't want anyone to know—not even you!" Then he got out his pig joke book and began to read them more of the jokes.

All at once Lisa yelled, "I know! I know what my carnival costume is going to be!" But she wouldn't tell Patti and D.J. what it was.

"Well, *my* costume is secret too!" said Patti.

7

After that there wasn't much more to say on the way home. They were all thinking about their secret costumes.

The week passed very slowly. Everyone at school was talking about their carnival costumes, but Lisa, Patti, and D.J. didn't say anything.

When the morning of the carnival came at last, they were all so happy they could hardly get their costumes on!

"Do you think I look fat enough?" asked Lisa. She patted her big pink tummy.

"You look as fat as a pig!" said her father. "Don't forget to take your skates."

Patti was getting make-up on at her house. Her mother put pink make-up all over her nose and then made a black line around it. It looked just like a pig's snout.

"Do you think I look funny enough to win?" asked Patti.

"*I'd* give you the prize," said her mother. "Now go on! You don't want to be late."

At D.J.'s house his mother was pinning together his costume. "Keep still, little pig," she laughed.

But D.J couldn't keep still. He wanted to go and show Lisa and Patti his costume. He was glad that he didn't have to keep his secret any more!

The three friends ran down the street to meet each other. But when they saw each other's costumes, they all stopped. "Oh, no! You're a pig too!" they all shouted.

"What funny costumes!" they all said together.

"Three pig costumes," said D.J. sadly. He knew that this had happened because of his joke book. "I just know the other kids are going to laugh at us!"

"I think we should all skate alone," said Patti.

They didn't say much the rest of the way. The carnival wasn't going to be much fun if they couldn't skate with their best friends!

When they got there, the skating rink looked beautiful. There were red and blue flags everywhere. All the kids were skating around the ice, shouting and laughing.

Patti, Lisa, and D.J. played games and skated with their other friends. It was fun, but not as much fun as if they had skated together.

At last it was time for the prizes. "This year's Funniest Costume Prize . . .," Miss Mason began. D.J., Patti, and Lisa skated near each other to listen. They heard Miss Mason say, ". . . goes to Bobby Hunt and his hot dog costume!"

11

12

Everyone laughed and cheered as Bobby skated around the ice.

"Well, I think you two look funnier," said D.J. "One of you should have got the prize."

"No, you should have," said Patti. "Or Lisa."

"And our Storybook People Prize," Miss Mason went on, "goes to Lisa, Patti, and D.J. who came to the carnival as . . . The Three Little Pigs!"

"Us?" said Lisa. "The Three Little Pigs?"

"Sure," said D.J. "Just look at us."

"Yaaa!!" yelled Patti. "A prize for the Green Street Three!"

They skated up together to get their prize as the other kids clapped and clapped. Patti smiled at D.J. "Good thing you got that joke book," she said.

Can't You Take a Joke?

Lisa was on her way to D.J.'s house when she met Patti. "What have you got there, Patti?" she asked.

"It's my new spy glass," said Patti. "Want to take a look?"

"Sure." Lisa looked through the spy glass. "I can't see a thing," she said.

"Really?" said Patti. "Try again."

Lisa looked, but she still couldn't see anything. "I don't think it's any good. You should take it back."

"Maybe I will," said Patti. "Thanks." Patti took back her spy glass and then she smiled a little smile to herself.

Then Patti met D.J. He had been looking for Lisa all morning. He asked Patti if she had seen her.

"I think she's gone to your house," Patti said.

D.J. was about to leave when he spotted the spy glass. He had never seen one before, so he asked Patti if he could take a look. He twisted and turned the spy glass this way and that, but he couldn't see through it. He handed it back.

"Too bad about your spy glass," he said. "See you, Patti."

As D.J. was leaving, Patti smiled another little smile to herself.

Lisa had been sitting on D.J.'s steps for a long time. Finally she spotted him coming down the street. She was about to ask where he had been when she saw his eye. He looked so funny that she began to laugh. But the odd thing was that *he* began to laugh at *her* too!

"What's so funny?" Lisa asked.

"Your eye!" said D.J. "It's got a black ring around it!"

"Well, so does yours!" she answered.

D.J. thought fast. "Patti! Patti and her spy glass!"

Rat-a-tat-tat. Patti went to answer her door. She knew it would be D.J. and Lisa. They would have found out about her trick by now. She hoped they wouldn't be too mad.

"That was some trick you pulled on us," said Lisa.

"It *was* funny, wasn't it?" said Patti. "We're still friends, aren't we?"

"Sure," said D.J. "Why not?"

"OK, shake," said Patti, so D.J. stuck out his hand.

Bzzzzzzz. D.J. let go and jumped back. Patti laughed. "How do you like my joke hand buzzer?" D.J. didn't answer. His hand was still feeling funny.

"Here," said Patti, handing Lisa a glass, "have something to drink."

"Yuck!" said Lisa, looking down into her glass. There was a fly in her ice cube!

Patti began to laugh. It was a trick ice cube.

"Let's go, Lisa," said D.J. He and Lisa turned and started walking to the door.

"Can't you two take a joke?" Patti asked.

But they didn't answer her. They just walked out. That night Patti had bad dreams. When she woke up she couldn't remember them, but she knew they were bad.

She was almost late for school that morning. All the children were at their desks when she got there. Lisa and D.J. smiled at her. Why were they being so friendly?

Patti looked at her desk. Could they have done something to it? Sure! They wanted to pay her back for those tricks she had pulled.

"You did something to my desk, didn't you?" she said to Lisa. Lisa shook her head.

"Patti, please sit down!" said Miss Mason. Patti sat down very slowly. Nothing happened! Lisa and D.J. just smiled.

At lunch, Patti put on Andy's hat and sat with her back to everyone. She hoped Lisa and D.J. wouldn't see her.

"Nice hat, Patti," called Lisa. "We've been looking for you."

D.J. was smiling. He had a white box in his hands. "We're sorry we got so mad at you about your tricks," he said.

"Yes," said Lisa. "We have something for you. Something good!"

"I know what it is!" said Patti. "It's a big black rat that jumps out when you take off the top!"

"What's she talking about?" Lisa asked D.J.

Patti watched as D.J. slowly took the top off the box. "I'm sorry I pulled those tricks on you," she said.

Lisa took out what looked like a cake. But what was it *really*?

"What's in it? Bugs?" Patti asked.

D.J. and Lisa shook their heads.

"OK then," said Patti, "you eat some."

D.J. and Lisa each took a bite of the cake. They seemed to like it.

"Eat some more," Patti said. Maybe there was something bad *inside* the cake.

They kept eating until half the cake was gone.

"Patti," said D.J., "please have some. We made it just for you."

Patti still didn't believe that there wasn't a trick in the cake. She made them keep eating. Finally, all that was left of the cake was one little bite.

"Come on, Patti," said Lisa, "have the last bite."

And Patti did. "Mmmmm," she said. "It's good!" She looked down at the empty plate. "I think I just tricked myself out of a cake!"

"Poor Patti!" said Lisa.

"No more tricks for me," said Patti.

A Cat for Lisa

By Nancy Prasad

"There's that cat again," said Lisa.

"What cat? Where?" D.J. asked.

"Over there. See?" said Lisa. A skinny orange cat was pawing through some rubbish.

"His owner doesn't feed him enough," D.J. said.

"I don't think he has an owner," said Lisa.

While the cat ate, he watched Lisa and D.J. When they came closer, he ran away.

"He looks so hungry," Lisa said sadly. She wanted so much to help the orange cat.

The next day Lisa took some money from her piggy bank and went to buy a tin of cat food. She put some of it in a small dish and took it to the place where the stray cat lived.

"Here, kitty, kitty," she called.

The orange cat peeped out from behind a dustbin. The food smelled good. The cat came halfway to Lisa. Then he ran away. Lisa could tell that he wasn't going to come over to the food as long as she was there. So she put the dish down and went home.

When she came back, the dish was empty and the cat was gone.

That night Lisa asked her dad if she could bring the cat home. She had never had a pet before, but she could see that this cat needed her. She had even picked out a name for him—Pumpkin—because he was orange.

"He's a stray," Lisa told her father. "No one cares about him."

"He may be a bit shy," Lisa's dad said. "It might be hard to bring him home."

"I can do it," Lisa said.

"All right, Lisa," said her dad. "You can have the cat."

Lisa hugged her dad as hard as she could. Tomorrow she would go to get the cat.

The next morning Lisa went over to Patti's house. Patti had a patch of catmint in her garden for her cat. Lisa asked for some.

"Why do you need catmint?" Patti asked. "You don't have a cat."

Lisa smiled. "I will have one soon."

Patti gave Lisa some catmint and her cat basket to bring Pumpkin home. Lisa put some catmint in the basket. She set the basket beside the dustbins and hid.

Pumpkin smelled the catmint. Then he ate a bit of it. Then he jumped into the basket.

"Hello, Pumpkin," said Lisa. "I caught you. You're my cat now." And she put the cover on the basket.

When they got home, Lisa lifted the lid. "This is your new home," she said. But Pumpkin hid in a corner of the basket.

Lisa put some milk in a dish. She put some dry food in another dish and some fish flakes on a plate. Then she sat down and watched.

After a while Pumpkin stuck his nose out of the basket. Then he slowly stepped out. He walked all around the room sniffing everything he saw.

Finally, he went over to the food. He ate every bit of it, and then he curled up to sleep. Lisa looked down at Pumpkin. Just watching him sleep made her feel all warm inside.

The next morning when Lisa fed Pumpkin, he rubbed against her legs.

"Oh Pumpkin," Lisa said. "I think you like me!" She held out her hand and let him sniff it. Then she patted him. He started purring.

After breakfast Pumpkin hid under Lisa's bed. When Lisa came into the room, he jumped on her foot.

Lisa could see that Pumpkin wanted to play. She got a ball and threw it to Pumpkin. He jumped on it and batted it across the rug.

28

Lisa scratched his chin. "You're a smart cat, Pumpkin!"

Pumpkin seemed to be getting bigger and bigger every day.

"This cat is getting fat," Lisa told her father. "Maybe I'm feeding him too much."

"Oh no!" said her dad. "Pumpkin's not fat and he's not a *he*. *She*'s going to have kittens!"

"Oh boy!" said Lisa. "More cats!"

Lisa's dad shook his head. "Too many cats, Lisa. We can't keep all of them. You'd better start thinking about what to do with the kittens."

One morning Lisa heard something under her bed. There was a small ball of fur moving around beside Pumpkin. It was crying.

"KITTENS!" cried Lisa and she called Patti and D.J. "Come on over!" she said. "Pumpkin's having her kittens NOW! UNDER MY BED!" Patti and D.J. went right over.

By noon, four small kittens were meowing and drinking milk from their mother.

"Soon I'll have to find homes for Pumpkin's kittens," Lisa said.

"Well, we can ask all the kids at school," Patti said.

So they asked everyone in their class if they wanted a kitten, but no one could take one. Next they tried putting up signs on the street, but no one called for a kitten.

It was then that D.J. thought of his aunt and uncle who had a farm. "They might have room for more cats. I'll ask."

So when Pumpkin's kittens were old enough, Lisa's dad drove Lisa, Patti, D.J., and the kittens out to the farm.

The house felt very empty when they got home. Lisa missed the kittens and she could tell that Pumpkin did too.

"We've still got each other," said Lisa, giving Pumpkin a hug.

"What about me?" asked Lisa's dad.

Lisa laughed. "And you too, Dad."

31

Journeys
Level Five
The Green Street Three

ART DIRECTOR/DESIGNER
Hugh Michaelson

TYPESETTING
PFB Art & Type Ltd.

FILM
Colourgraph Reproduction
Systems Inc.

PRINTING
Chorley & Pickersgill Ltd.